Disco

DISCOVERING
CELTIC CUISINE

Margaret Rees

Illustrations by
David Manton

First Impression – 2002

ISBN 1 84323 079 8

Printed in Wales by
Gomer Press, Llandysul, Ceredigion

I should like to acknowledge the especial influence on this book of the work of
Gretel Beer, Darina Allen, Anne Willan, Lady Llanover, Bobby Freeman,
and historians John Davies and Peter Beresford Ellis.

Generations of cooks, teachers, writers,
professional chefs, food and wine producers,
family and friends have passed on to me their skills and knowledge.

This book is dedicated to them.

NOTE ON THE AUTHOR AND PHOTOGRAPHER

Margaret Rees is a pioneer of the emerging tastes of Wales and a noted authority on Welsh food. An award-winning former chef and restaurateur, her culinary talents have brought her many prizes and recommendations, including *The Sunday Times* Taste of Britain award and listings in Les Routiers and Good Food Guides. She is a member of the International Association of Culinary Professionals.

David Manton graduated in 1986 with a BA Honours Degree in Photographic Design, and subsequently worked as a photographer in New Jersey, USA. On his return to the UK he settled in Cardiff with his wife Joanne, and in 1990 they set up The Photodrome Limited, an advertising photography studio. The Photodromes's many clients include British Airways, Hoover Candy, WDA, National Assembly for Wales, Hyder and SWALEC.

Both Margaret Rees and David Manton have approached the creation of this book as an artistic collaboration, and intend to work together on many similar projects in the future.

Contents

The Celtic heartland in pre-Christian times

Introduction

As far back as I can remember, food has played an important part in my life. I grew up in a coalmining village in west Wales. Adventures with cooking started at my grandmother's apron strings in her old-fashioned kitchen around the end of the Second World War. Money and food were both in short supply, so we grew, harvested and cooked our own food. It was organic, fresh, clean and unadulterated. We supplemented this with food gathered liberally from the hedgerows: fruits, flowers and herbs. The recipes that we used were simple and wholesome: *cawl* (a traditional Welsh soup), breads, cakes, preserves and wines. I have since learned that similar food customs and recipes were associated with the homes of working people throughout Europe.

During my student days in the 60s, I took a cooking course in the tiny saltmining village of Hallstadt in Austria. I was later to discover that this area is known as the Cradle of the Celts in Europe. Whilst there, I learned about the local Austrian food traditions. I spent a night in the village bakery, for example, learning how to bake traditional breads and strudels. My apprenticeship in Herr Zauner's hotel kitchen was a daily culinary adventure. Thirty years later, after a career as a teacher, restaurateur and broadcaster, circumstances led me back to Austria to live and work. I ran a holiday business combining my interests in food, wine and skiing – a wonderful combination! My visits to food and wine producers in the area gave me the opportunity to share local people's knowledge of their food and traditions. My Austrian friends and neighbours still relate to their *keltische* roots through such seasonal customs as the ancient pagan parades of the *Krampus* which begin at Advent.

I later developed an interest in my Celtic heritage more generally, which led me back to places I had already visited, and also to investigate new locations. I discovered that the small villages of Hallstadt and its neighbour Hallein were on the culinary crossroads of Europe in Austria from ancient Celtic times. The food chain that I unearthed led me throughout Europe on my quest for good food.

*　　　*　　　*

Evidence of a significant Celtic settlement dates from the eighth century BC at

Hallstadt. This is an area of such archaeological importance that its name has been adopted to refer to the first Iron Age more generally, now known as the Hallstadt Culture. The village itself developed around the salt mines there. Salt became a staple of the Celts' economy, and was in great demand as a food preservative and taste enhancer. Austria was a centre of European trade routes, and Celtic traders took salt over the Alps from Hallstadt to the cities of Greece and Italy, and they also transported their goods along the great European rivers the Danube, Rhine, Elbe, Rhone, Seine and Po. It is along these trade routes that we can still find fascinating evidence of their ancient settlements.

The Celts were pastoral peoples, successful farmers and traders, and population growth led them to seek new land. They were fierce fighters, although they did not have a common ruler. At their strongest by 300 BC, they dominated much of Europe. Their lands ranged from Britain and Ireland in the north to France and Spain in the south and east as far as the Balkans and Turkey. Their unity came from a set of dialects based on a common language and a shared culture. By the second century BC the Romans and the Germanic tribes were challenging them.

In the absence of a written language, the history of the ancient Celts lies in their artefacts and in the writings of the ancient Greeks and Romans. Yet their influence in Europe is strong. It lives on in its languages, place names and traditions. For me, as a food historian, part of their living heritage lies in our food culture.

Celtic cooking traditionally took place in a cauldron over an open fire. The hearth was the centre of their one-roomed homes, and it provided both heat and light for cooking. The significance of the cauldron is seen in the magical association with which it is endowed in mythology, featuring frequently, for example, as a symbol of abundance or renewal.

The Celtic cauldron could be used for boiling meat or heating drinks. Some of the foods that are known to have formed their staple diet included spelt, wheat, barley, rye and oats, pork, beef, lamb and wild boar; fish, eggs, honey, cabbage, leeks, beans, peas, lentils and seaweeds.

Feasts and celebrations were important to the tribal Celts. These festivals were first identified on the Coligny Calendar, an inscribed bronze disc which was found near Lyon in France in1897. It featured the largest number of ancient Celtic words ever found on an artefact, which introduced and identified the lunar and solar calendars used by the Celts and their Fire Feasts.

Samhain, the Celtic New Year, was celebrated on 1st November. This was the most important day in the Celtic year, as it was the time when animals were brought in from grazing, and when some were slaughtered in order to provide food for the winter. Feasting started at dusk on 31st October, and marked the time between the death of the old year and the start of the new year at dawn. Being neither of the new year nor the old year, *Samhain* was thought to be an especially magical time. In Christian times *Samhain* was replaced by All Saints or All Hallows Day. The evening before it has become known as Halloween.

Imbolc was celebrated on 1st February, marking the lambing season, and also the time of year when a plentiful supply of ewes' milk was available for making cheese.

Beltane was celebrated on the 1st May, marking the time when cattle were sent out to graze again. It was seen as a time of growth, when the sun was moving into the summer solstice. Fires were lit to purify the air and safeguard the fertility of people and livestock.

Lughnasad, on 1st August, celebrated the time when crops were beginning to ripen, auguring well for the harvest that lay ahead. In Scotland they call this *Lammas*, or *Loafmas*.

Seasonal feasts were associated with particular foods, such as bannock. The apple, for example, was the Celtic symbol of fertility, while the salmon represented wisdom. The goose was revered for the vigilance it symbolised, and the wild boar was representative of the warrior spirit.

*   *   *

It seems that my Welsh background and all my training and experience in the food industry have led full circle to a wider appreciation of my heritage, in its full Celtic perspective. It is this that I want to share with people in *Discovering Celtic Cuisine*. I have compiled a selection of traditional recipes from European countries with Celtic connections. The recipes are linked by the similarities of the older cooking methods and ingredients which survive into modern times. I have tried to show how they can be given a contemporary interpretation. However, in doing this, I have attempted to avoid sacrificing the value of real food for the sake of fashion. Real food has its roots in our past. Real food is instantly recognisable by its elemental warmth. It delights by its surprise, and appeals to all the senses. Recreating a recipe from the past is like translating poetry – it can be done, but it will never be exactly the same as the original. It requires a combination of imagination and restraint to make the recipes relevant to our requirements today. I have tried to produce recipes for today that retain the taste of their origins and are without pretension. The recipes, accompanied by David Manton's stylish photographs, are meant to inspire another generation to cook real food, food that nurtures. I hope that they are recipes that you will enjoy and want to use again.

Margaret Rees

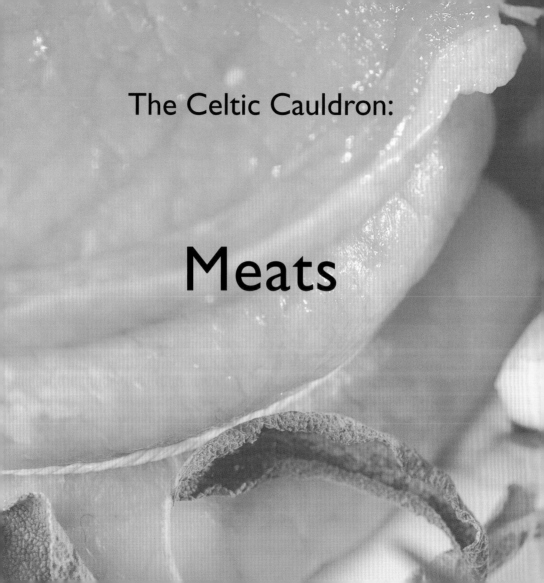

The Celtic Cauldron:

Meats

The popularity of cauldron cooking across the Celtic countries has resulted in a large number of variations on this dish, from Welsh cawl to Manx broth (see page 4 for further details).

Tafelspitz is the famous Austrian dish named after the cut of beef from the upper leg of the animal. Cooked in the broth, the meat is served in thick slices cut across the fibres and served with either fresh creamed apple and horseradish or sour cream and chive sauce. This is delicious eaten with mixed vegetables from the soup.

ONE POT COOKING

Ingredients are very similar for all the classic peasant broths and stocks across the Celtic European countries.

Ingredients

1 kilo cuts of stewing meats, such as lamb, mutton, beef or ham, pork, wild boar, venison
1 kilo mixed herbs and root vegetables, e.g. swede, turnips, parsnips, carrots, leeks, potatoes, lovage, celeriac, parsley
Various garnishes for regional soups such as pearl barley, flour, eggs, *knödel* (dumplings)
2.5 litres of water

Method

The meat and vegetables are boiled slowly for 2-3 hours. The meat is then lifted out, and the vegetables can also be strained, leaving a clear, aromatic and nutritious broth to which any chosen garnish can be added.

Serves 6-8

Follow these quantities for all variations on this dish shown overleaf.

Welsh cawl

Welsh cawl is made with lamb and/or beef.
Occasionally ham is also added. Vegetables
normally used to make this dish include
carrots, parsnips and swede. Garnish with 1
finely shredded leek and 1 tbsp parsley.

Scotch broth

Use a neck of lamb, and add 1 tbsp each
of dried peas and pearl barley to the basic
mixture, adding 1 small shredded cabbage
as a garnish.

Manx Broth

Add dumplings to the basic broth. These are
very easy to make: simply combine 100g
flour, 25g butter, 25g parsley and water; shape
into small rounds and place in the boiling
broth to cook for 4-5 minutes.

Breton pot au feu

Use beef as your basic meat for this dish. Add
¼ tsp grated nutmeg, 2 cloves of garlic, 1 stick
of celery and 1 shredded small cabbage to the
basic mixture.

LEBERKNÖDEL SOUP

Follow the basic beef broth recipe, adding the liver dumplings, which are made as follows: Soak 3 dry bread rolls or thick slices of bread in water, then squeeze and drain. Add 1 tsp of gently fried chopped onion and blend well with 175g of minced lamb or pig's liver (a food processor can be used to do this). Add 1 egg and a 1 tsp mixture of chopped herbs such as parsley, thyme and marjoram. Leave to stand and then shape into small rounds the size of a walnut, using dry breadcrumbs. These can be deep or shallow fat fried, and then dropped into the broth as a garnish.

FAGGOTS

Faggots are made by mincing 450g liver and 25g pork fat, and then combining with 225g breadcrumbs and 225g finely chopped onions. Shape tablespoonfuls of the mixture into rounds to form a faggot. Traditionally, these would have been wrapped in caul fat. Place in a greased tin, cook in the oven at 175°C for 35-45 minutes. Serve with cooked dried peas. *Caillettes*, as they are known in France, are made by adding two cloves of garlic to the above recipe and 250g lightly steamed chopped spinach.

The *pot-au-feu* family can be cooked classic-style in an earthenware pot, or in a pressure cooker or heavy iron casserole. It calls for a simple classic approach – balancing the flavours, poaching and, of course, skimming away the fat. The flavour is derived from the tougher parts of meat which have more gelatine, and cuts which have some marrowbone. A boned chicken stuffed with pork can be cooked in this way to make a *galatine*.

POTÉE (from France)

This is a fundamental Gaulic cauldron dish – the richer, heavier pork version of the beef *pot-au-feu*. Regional provincial styles proliferate, from *hochepot*, a classic from Flanders, to *poulet-au-pot* from Bern in Switzerland.

Ingredients to make the stock

2-3 kilos salted or fresh bacon, ham, hocks or pork, 1 onion studded with cloves, 1 bunch mixed fresh wild herbs or bouquet garni, 10 black peppercorns, 1 stick celery, 1 bay leaf, 1 kilo mixed diced root vegetables, 1 leek and 1 green cabbage, 5 litres cold water

Method

All the stock ingredients are placed in a large saucepan and simmered for 2-3 hours. Strain and chill at this stage to remove excess fat from the surface. The root vegetables are then cooked in the stock for 30 minutes until tender. The leek and cabbage are cooked for 10 minutes. All vegetables are strained and arranged with sliced meats on a warm deep serving dish. As a main course, serve with a choice of mustards, gherkin pickles or horseradish.

The strained broth is reduced for the first course. 100g noodles can be added to cook for 5 minutes before serving, or dumplings stuffed with cabbage leaves can be cooked in the broth. Add to main course.

Welsh Salt duck

Lady Llanover wrote the book *First Principles of Good Cookery* in the middle of the nineteenth century and is renowned for her interest in recording interesting Welsh cultural customs for posterity, from costumes to recipes. Her Welsh salt duck recipe has retained its popularity, and is used by many top chefs today. This dish is similar to French *confit*.

Ingredients

Free-range organic Barbary duck 4-5lbs in weight
125g sea salt, such as the popular Anglesey salt, *Halen Môn*
2 large onions

Method

Wipe the duck inside and out with kitchen paper. Place in a large bowl and rub all over with the salt. Leave for a few days, turning the duck daily. Rinse with cold water. Place into a large pot, add onions and cover with cold water, bring to the boil and simmer for 2 hours.

Purée the onions into a sauce, using a liquidizer or passing through a sieve. Thin out by adding stock. Serve the duck with the sauce and a selection of fresh vegetables.

Serves 4-6

To preserve the duck French confit-style, cook as salt duck (right). Cut into joints and place in an earthenware crock or glass preserving jar. Strain the stock and clarify the fat. Add 250g of pure lard and pour over the joints, ensuring that they are well covered. Further layers of the duck and lard can be added the next day. Seal, cover with greaseproof paper and a tight-fitting lid. The preserve can be kept for months, and the fat used to fry Hungarian cabbage, wild mushrooms and potatoes. Individual joints of the preserved duck can be fried or roasted in the oven to reheat (15-20 minutes).

This is a traditional Alpine dish, made using home-cured and smoked meats, as well as leftover pork and beef. Wild mushrooms are added when in season. In Wales, this dish is simply known as *cig moch a winwns*, and consists of potatoes, ham and onions.

Ingredients

> 100g diced smoked or cured ham or bacon (*Speck*),
>   with beef and pork as optional additions
> 25g chopped onions
> 200g diced firm cooked potatoes
> 4 eggs, fried
> parsley to garnish

Method

> Gently fry the *Speck* for 4 minutes and then add the onions. Once the onions are lightly cooked, then add the optional diced cooked meats. Boil in strips, dice and add the potatoes, and fry the mixture until browned.

Traditionally this dish is served in the frying pan on a wooden stand either individually or in a very large family-sized pan. Fried eggs (1 per person) are placed on top. A blini pan is an ideal size for serving individual portions of this dish as a side dish.

*a tin filled with 2 inches of water

BRETON COUNTRY PORK PÂTÉ

Ingredients

> 500g each of liver and belly pork, 250g bacon, 2 twigs each of sage, thyme and rosemary and bay leaves, 5 fl oz wine or brandy, seasoning

Method

> Mix the diced liver and belly pork, season and marinade in wine overnight. Line an ovenproof dish with the thinly sliced streaky bacon. Pour the meat mixture into the dish and top with the belly pork fat or skin, bay leaves and herbs. Seal the dish and cook in a bain-marie* in a moderate oven (160°C) for 3-4 hours.

COCK-A-LEEKIE

This Scottish dish is a typical peasant-style dish, originating from the tradition of committing the old hens to the table when they have finished laying. Each European Celtic country offers its own twist on this dish, whether it be cooking time or the addition of further ingredients.

Ingredients

1 large boiling fowl (1.5-2 kilos), 3.5 litres water, 1 tsp salt, 1 tsp peppercorns, 2.5 kilos of leeks cut into short lengths. Optional additions: 1 kilo potatoes, 250g prunes or raisins.

Method

Wipe the chicken and place in a boiling crock (or pressure cooker), cover with salted water and crushed peppercorns and simmer for 30 minutes. Add half the leeks and cook for 90 minutes. Add the rest of the leeks and cook for a further 30 minutes. Potatoes can be added at this stage if desired. Serve as a two-part meal – soup stock thickened with leek and then the chicken, cut into pieces, with potatoes. Adjust all cooking times and the liquid if using the pressure cooker.

Serves 6-8

The soup is sometimes thickened with finely ground oatmeal. Prunes or raisins can be added 30 minutes before the end of cooking time in order to sweeten the dish.

Roasting the bird after boiling adds a special taste – the modern cooking method could involve the use of a pressure cooker for quick results. To pot roast the chicken Romanian-style, scatter 15-20 peeled and sliced garlic cloves over the chicken and place a knob of butter inside. Place it in a baking dish and pour 150ml of cream over it. Cover with foil or a close-fitting lid. Roast for 30 minutes at 200°C. Serve with noodles and salad.

The Celtic Cauldron:

Fish

CULLEN SKINK

This is a Scottish fish soup. The soup or broth can be made with meat, fish or even a sheep's head, simmered with cereal. Cullen is the name of the fishing village in the north-east of Scotland where this recipe first originated.

Fish soups and stews are simple and delightful when cooked from a variety of fresh fish and shellfish, with the mixture used depending on the catch of the day. The *bouillabaisse* of Marseille, for example, is similar to the Cornish and Breton *cotriande* featured over the page.

Ingredients

750 diced potatoes
2 diced onions
500g natural smoked Finnan haddock
900ml milk
seasoning
50g flour
50g butter
cream and chive garnish

Method

Cover the haddock and onions with milk and poach for 5-6 minutes. Lift the fish from the stock, and remove the skin and any bones. Then flake the fish coarsely. Put the potatoes to cook in the milk stock with the onions for 10 minutes. Mash or liquidize and add most of the fish to the skink. Season to taste. Add a drizzle of cream and chive to the finished skink. To serve, sprinkle on the remaining fish flakes as a final flourish.

Welsh mussel stew and Breton *moules marinières* are made by stewing cleaned, closed mussels in water and wine with herbs until they open. Cream is added to the Welsh version.

Fish goulash recipes originated along the banks of the Danube. Prepare as for *cotriande bretonne* (right), leaving out the mussels and adding two skinned de-seeded tomatoes and a finely diced green pepper, 1 tbsp sweet paprika and a swirl of sour cream.

COTRIANDE BRETONNE

This is a delicious fish stew made with with sorrel and leek.

Ingredients

750g each of rich fish and white fish, boned and filleted, 1 litre fish stock, 800ml cleaned mussels, 500g sorrel (raw or canned), 60g butter, 500g potatoes thinly sliced, 2 each of finely chopped onions, leeks and cloves, seasoning, 300ml double cream or crème fraiche, large 2-3 litre cooking pot, 10ml white wine, a dash of white wine vinegar

Method

Fish stock: Bone, fillet and skin all fish and eels. Boil in 1 litre water with herbs, a piece of onion and the garlic. Add a splash of wine vinegar and the white wine.

Soup: Cut the fish into 5cm pieces and wipe dry with kitchen paper. Clean the mussels, removing the wiry beards. Discard any that are open. Melt the butter in a large pan and add onions, garlic and leeks. Cook gently for 2-3 minutes: do not brown. Add the fish stock, seasoning and potatoes and simmer for 5 minutes until potatoes are slightly cooked.

Add the rich fish and simmer for 5 minutes before adding the white fish, sorrel, cream and the mussels in their shells. Continue simmering until the mussels open. Adjust seasoning and serve from the cooking pot.

Salmon in a Leek Wrap

Salmon was regarded as the fish of wisdom by the ancient Celts. Leek has a subtle onion flavour. Both salmon and leek are used all over Europe: in fact only two green vegetables merit a mention in the ancient Welsh Laws of Hywel Dda – the leek and the cabbage.

Welsh, Scottish and Irish salmon is baked or poached with wild herbs and sometimes served with wild sorrel or fennel sauce. Brittany salmon is poached in Muscadet from the vineyards of the Loire at Nantes. A sauce is made from the local salty butter – *beurre salé* – which is a strong yellow colour with a cheesy taste. Combined with shallots, it makes a wonderful classic sauce called *beurre blanc* – delicious served with pike and salmon.

Ingredients

4 x 100g fillets boned salmon, 4 long leek leaves, 100ml dry white wine, water to cover

Method

Parcel-wrap a leek leaf around each salmon fillet. Place these in a saucepan or steamer and cover with cold salted water and add the wine. Slowly bring to the boil and cook for two minutes. Turn off the heat, but leave the fish in the stock for five minutes to finish cooking. Serve hot with a sauce (such as laverbread, gooseberry or fennel), boiled new potatoes or cold with a salad.

For a laverbread sauce recipe, see page 26.

PAN-FRIED TROUT IN OATMEAL

There is an excellent stock of river fish to be had right across Europe, such as rainbow and brown trout, saibling, char, carp, pike, sewin and sea trout, from which this dish can be made.

Ingredients

1 medium trout per person
25g oatmeal per trout
oil and butter for frying
seasoning

Method

Descale, cut and wipe fish dry. Coat with oatmeal. Fry in hot oil and butter for 3-4 minutes on both sides. Check if the flesh falls away from the bone. (The fish can also be baked in the oven for 15-20 minutes, depending on size.)

Wrapping small delicate fish in home-cured ham, bacon or leek leaves, or coating in oatmeal as in this recipe, both protects the fish when cooking and imparts an interesting flavour.

BLUE TROUT

When you plunge a really fresh trout into a pan full of boiling water, flavoured with green herbs and vinegar, it will immediately turn blue. Turn the heat to very low, simmer for just three minutes, and stand for two minutes. Serve garnished with fresh fennel or dill. This is a very popular way of cooking fish in Hallstadt in Austria and also in Germany.

CORNISH FISH-GAZY PIE

Savoury and sweet pies and pasties feature in the culinary history of many countries, and they can be cooked as single portions or as family-sized treats. This fish recipe can make an appetizing and unusual starter baked in individual dishes. Manx herrings with *Priddhas* is a similarly tasty combination of fish and potato.

The rocky Celtic seashore produces sand eels, limpets, whelks, periwinkles, and mussels. Cockles live in the sand, while laverbread, kelp, carrageen and marsh samphire are gathered from the seashore. The ancient peasant favoured such wild foods, as they cost nothing. Many are still available today if we take the time to pick, gather, fish and hunt.

Ingredients

Shortcrust pastry (for recipe see page 47), 6 pilchards or herrings or small mackerel, 50g breadcrumbs, 100ml cream, parsley, 4 eggs, 3 uncooked potatoes, few drops vinegar

Method

Take a large oval pie dish. Slice or grate potatoes onto the base. Place the prepared gutted fish – with the head and tail still on – in a ring with the heads in the centre and the tail to the sides of the dish. Season and sprinkle with vinegar. Beat the eggs and cream and pour over the fish. Roll out and cut pastry to cover the dish and poke the heads and tail out to create a dramatic presentation. Bake in a moderate 210°C oven for 25 minutes.

Instead of the large pie dish, small oval dishes can be used to serve individual portions.

PENCLAWDD COCKLE PIE

Ingredients

Shortcrust pastry – see appendix for recipe
(alternatively, mashed potatoes and cheese can be
used instead of pastry)
500g cockles in shell
225g streaky bacon, diced
2 onions or shallots, chopped

Method

Boil cockles in salted water with a little oatmeal,
until opened. Remove the meat from the shell and
layer in a shallow dish. Cook the streaky bacon, add
onions and cook until transluscent. Sprinkle over the
cockles, cover with shortcrust pastry or potatoes and
cheese. Bake in the oven at 200°C for 15-20 minutes
until golden brown.

Ancient fishing ports are to be
found around the coasts of
Cornwall, Wales, the Isle of Man
and Scotland. Pembrokeshire's
herring catch was traditionally at
its best in autumn, and historical
texts on the area mention
bottlenose whales, porpoises and
blue sharks, which were deemed
especially useful for their
considerable supply of oil.
Whalemeat was dried, salted and
smoked for Lent.

Galway Bay oysters

Oysters are considered to be in their prime when there is an 'r' in the month. A wild, exotic food, it is renowned for its qualities as an aphrodisiac: the Irish love theirs washed down with stout.

Method

Discard any that are even slightly open. Hold the oyster in a small towel and, using a strong oyster knife, place it under the hinge side and then with a sharp twist of the knife separate the shells. Run the knife under the oyster in the deep shell flipping it over. Save the delicious juice in the shell and garnish with fresh wedges of lemon.

Brown soda bread makes a wonderful accompaniment to these luxurious foods.

CARP FOR CHRISTMAS EVE IN AUSTRIA

Prepare the live carp by leaving it in clean fresh water for 2 days to remove the river or pond mud. The carp may be baked whole with herbs or slices dipped in egg and breadcrumbs and fried. Lemon and potato salad should be served.

Laverbread Sauce

Ingredients

100g laverbread, 100ml fish wine cooking stock (which will be left over from the salmon recipe on page 18, for example)
60-100g double cream (optional addition)
seasoning

Method

Place all the ingredients in a saucepan. Stir and simmer for 3-4 minutes. Adjust texture, adding more stock instead of cream if a lighter sauce is preferred. To cook in a microwave, place all ingredients in a basin and cook for two minutes. Stir well. Serve with the fish.

Laverbread Dishes

Edible seaweeds include laverbread (Wales), kelp (Scotland) and carrogeen moss (Ireland). These are all an excellent source of nutrition, and are used to make sauces to accompany meat and fish.

A typical Welsh miner's breakfast consisted of home-cured bacon, egg and laverbread, coated in medium-fine oatmeal and fried in the bacon fat.

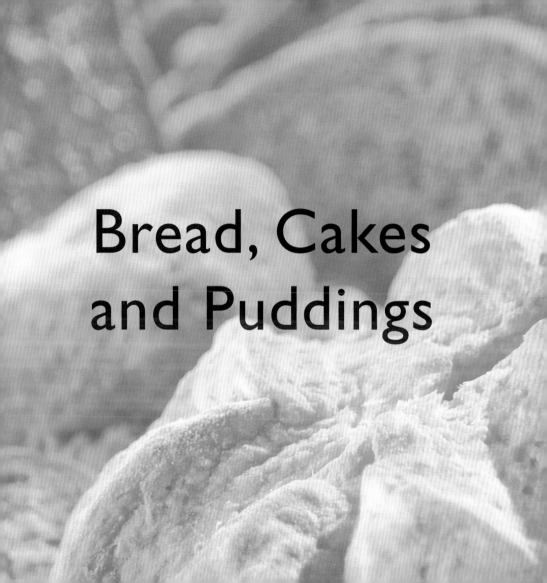

Bread, Cakes
and Puddings

BASIC BREAD RECIPE

Ingredients

900g breadmaking flour of your choice
1 tbsp fresh yeast or 2 tsp dried yeast
a pinch of salt
1 tbsp oil, butter, or lard
warm water to mix

Method

To prepare the yeast, mix with a little sugar and allow to froth in a small bowl. If making a sour dough leavening, prepare beforehand. Dried yeast can be added directly to the flour according to the directions on the packet.

Weigh up all the dry ingredients. Place the chosen flour or mixture of flour in a warm bowl. Add the creamed or dried yeast or a quantity of sour dough starter, also the other ingredients. Make the soft dough by mixing with the melted fats or oil and warm water. Shape into a round and cut a cross on the top.

Put the bowl containing the mixture in a warm place, covering it with a large oiled polythene bag, and tie loosely. When it has risen to approximately twice its size, draw the mixture together and knead well. Cut into the desired shape and place into tins to prove until they double their size once again (after approximately 1 hour).

Bake in the oven at 180°C-200°C. An average-sized loaf will take up to 40 minutes, while bread rolls take 10-15 minutes. Tap the loaf to check if it is cooked.

Home-made yeast was first developed to make leavened bread or Continental sour dough starter. *Barm* (Ireland, Cornwall) *berem* or *burum* (Welsh), sometimes known as temperance yeast, is made using boiled mashed potato, flour and sugar mixed with water. It is then poured into a bottle or wide-topped jar and left to ferment. Raisins or hops can be added to activate fermentation, which is facilitated by covering the top loosely.

BARA CRAI Welsh Soda Bread

675g brown wholemeal flour, 450g strong white flour, 1 tsp salt, 2 tsp bicarbonate of soda, 750ml buttermilk/ milk

Method
Sieve all the dry ingredients into a bowl and mix into a non-sticky dough with the buttermilk. Flour and gently shape into a 5cm round. Place on a floured baking sheet and mark into quarters with a knife. Cook at 210°C for 35-40 minutes, or until the bread sounds hollow when tapped. Cut and serve warm with butter.

BARA BRITH

Bara brith means 'speckled bread' in Welsh.

Take 500g of proven basic bread dough and add a handful of mixed fruit, 125g sugar and 1 tsp mixed spice. Either bake in a loaf tin, or as a round on a flat baking sheet. For baking instructions, see the basic bread recipe.

POTATO BREAD

Ingredients

500g boiled mashed potatoes, 100g flour
50g sugar, 25g butter, 25g currants, milk to
mix

Method

Add butter to hot mashed potatoes, sugar,
currants and flour. Add a little milk as
required to make a soft dough. Roll and cut
or shape in rounds, and cook on a griddle
on both sides until golden brown.

WELSH CAKES

Ingredients

250g plain flour plus ½ tsp baking powder
or self-raising flour, 125g margarine, butter
or lard, 120g currants, 1 large egg and a
little milk, pinch of mixed spice or nutmeg

Method

Rub the fat into the flour and spice, add all
the dry ingredients and mix a little milk
with the egg to make a soft dough. Roll out
on a floured board to a ¼" thickness. Cut
into 2-3 inch rounds. Bake on a lightly
greased, moderately hot iron bakestone, or
non-stick griddle.

Zelten is made at the beginning of Advent, and stored until Christmas Eve. The last slice should be eaten before the last day of January. It is traditional during Advent to serve the *Zelten* buttered and thinly sliced to any guests with a glass of warm *Glühwein*. A seasonal celebration decoration can be added (as in the photograph opposite) by topping with a mixture of dried fruits, walnuts and melted honey.

ZELTEN CELEBRATION BREAD

Austrian Christmas bread from the Tyrol

Ingredients

1 kg dried figs, ½ kg each of sultanas and almonds, 125g each of pine nuts, candied lemon peel, mixed peel, hazelnuts, walnuts and raisins, 250g dates or dried plums, 1 level tsp cinnamon and cloves, juice of 1-2 lemons, 18 fl oz dark rum (*Stroh*), 9 fl oz brandy, rye bread dough (made of 800g rye flour, 18 fl oz tepid water, 40g fresh yeast, salt)

Method

Coarsely chop all nuts and fruits and mix with the spice. Add all the other ingredients and leave to stand for 12 hours. Prepare the bread dough, following the basic recipe on page 28. Combine the marinaded fruit mixture with the dough, kneading well, and shape into oblongs 18-20cm long by 4-5cm thick. Set on a buttered baking sheet and leave to rise for 30-50 minutes (until they double their size). Bake for 10 minutes at 220°C, then lower the temperature and cook for a further 50 minutes. The breads can be brushed with a light honey liquid, and stored for 2-3 weeks before slicing and eating.

In some areas flour and water paste are mixed together and wrapped around the cakes before baking.

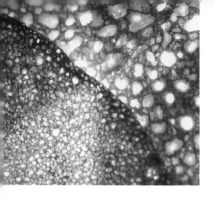

CELTIC PANCAKES

Breton galettes

Ingredients

250g buckwheat flour, 260 g plain flour, 10g salt, 600ml milk, 300ml approx. water, 125g clarified butter, oil for griddle

Method

Sift the flours and salt into a large bowl, gradually adding half the milk, beat well and then add the remaining milk. Leave to stand for 30-40 minutes. Add water and beat the batter until it feels thick and creamy. Add half the clarified butter and repeat the process. The mixture can be beaten quite easily by using a liquidiser or an electric whisk.

To fry, heat either a special iron crêpe pan or non-stick frying pan and brush with oil and melted butter. Wipe clean with oiled kitchen paper. Ladle approximately 2-3 tablespoons of the batter onto the hot surface, tilting the pan until it is covered very thinly. Use a special traditional wooden rake or the back of a ladle to spread. Allow to cook quickly and turn when golden speckled brown and set. Turn and stack onto a paper towel and continue to wipe the pan between frying each *galette*. Add more water if batter is too thick. Do not overcook, as they will be reheated with the filling inside.

Serve with sweet or savoury fillings such as eggs, ham, cheese, sardines, sausages.

The Breton *galettes* should be cooked lacy and crisp. They are the traditional bread of Brittany, and are used as a wrap for many different savoury and sweet fillings. Sometimes they are cut into strips and put into soups, in Austria for example.

Buckwheat was traditionally the flour of the poor, and had an earthy taste. Richer mixtures made with eggs and wheat flour are usually called crêpes.

IRISH BOXTY PANCAKES

Ingredients

225g each of freshly cooked potatoes, peeled raw potatoes and white flour, ¾ tsp bicarbonate of soda, 225-350ml buttermilk, seasoning, oil and butter for frying

Method

Mash the hot cooked potatoes and grate the raw potatoes into the bowl, add the flour, soda and seasoning. Mix well with the buttermilk to make a firm batter. Cook on a flat heated griddle or frying pan. Traditionally the pancakes are eaten with crisp bacon rashers or honey.

WELSH PANCAKES

Ingredients

450g plain strong flour, 1 tsp each of fresh or dried yeast and sugar, 2 tbsp oil, 500ml water and milk, a pinch of salt

Method

Combine sugar, yeast, warm milk and water. Gradually add half the liquid to the flour. Beat well, then add the rest of the liquid. Cover the bowl with a plastic bag; and leave for 1 hour. Beat again and stand for a further 30 minutes. Cook table-spoonfuls of the mixture on a hot griddle. Turn and cook to a light golden brown.

AUSTRIAN PANCAKES
(Palatschinken)

Ingredients

140g plain flour, 1-2 eggs, 250ml milk,
melted butter or oil for frying

Method

Sieve the flour into the bowl and add the
beaten eggs and add enough milk to mix into a
thin batter. Heat a greased medium-sized
frying pan, and when hot pour a thin layer
of batter into the pan. Tilt and allow to set,
turn and cook to a golden brown. Stack one
on top of each other to keep warm. Serve
with sweet or savoury fillings.

PANCAKE TERRINE

A pancake terrine can be made by layering
pancakes with vegetables in a cream sauce
alternately with cooked ham, chicken, turkey
or fish, lasagne-style. The top layer should be
covered with grated or crumbled firm cheese.
A recipe for a suitable cream sauce can be
found on page 47 in the appendix.

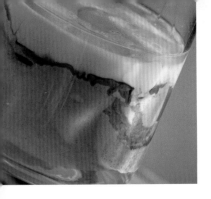

Topfen Palatschinken

This is a delicious Austrian recipe for pancakes filled with curd cheese.

Ingredients

6-8 pancakes (follow recipe for Austrian pancakes on page 36)

Filling

200g curd cheese, 40g each of butter, caster sugar and raisins, a little rum, 2 eggs, 120ml sour cream, 1 tsp vanilla sugar or pure vanilla essence, 1 grated lemon zest, a pinch of cinnamon

Topping

140ml sour cream, 2 tbsp milk, 1 egg
30g icing sugar

Method

Soak the raisins in a little Austrian rum to swell. Separate the eggs, cream together the butter, egg yolks, sugar, sour cream and curd cheese. Add the grated lemon zest, vanilla sugar and cinnamon and raisins. Whisk the egg whites until stiff and fold into the mixture. Spread half of each pancake with the mixture, roll up and place in an ovenproof dish. Whisk together the topping mixture and pour over the pancakes. Cook at oven temperature 180°C for 25 minutes until custard has set. Serve warm, dusted with icing sugar.

The tradition of the Lenten food feast survives to the present day right across Europe in some form or other, from the traditions of St Bridget's Day in Ireland to the *Fashing* or Carnival time of Central and Eastern Europe. In Austria one of the most popular dishes for this time of year is *Fashing Krapfen* – doughnuts filled with apricot jam. All these customs encompass the ancient Celtic festival of *Imbolc* on 1st February which celebrates the first day of spring and the beginning of a new year on the farm.

APFELSTRUDEL

Ingredients

700g tart apples
2 tbsp raisins
75g butter
50g flour
1 tsp ground cinnamon
juice and zest of 1 lemon
40g soft dry fine white breadcrumbs
75g slivered almonds

STRUDEL TEIG (Pastry)

1 tbsp olive oil
125g strong flour
warm water
vinegar

Place the flour, salt, oil and a drop of wine vinegar or lemon juice in a bowl or food processor. Add sufficient warm water to make a soft elastic dough. Remove from bowl and shape. Brush with oil, cover with a plastic bag and leave for half an hour to rest.

Alternatively, bought filo pastry can be used.

Method

Place 50g of the butter in a saucepan, melt, and add the breadcrumbs until brown. Peel, core and finely slice or grate the apple and sprinkle with lemon juice. Melt the remaining butter. Spread a large white cloth over the kitchen table, dust with flour and roll out the pastry as thinly as possible. Work the dough from underneath with the hands, extending it over the edge of the table. Brush the dough with melted butter and then spread with the breadcrumbs. Arrange the fruit on top with raisins, cinnamon and almonds. Lift the cloth and roll the *strudel* like a Swiss roll. Seal the ends and roll on to a large baking sheet lined with parchment paper. Shape into a crescent and brush with the rest of the melted butter. Bake at oven temperature 220°C for 15 minutes. Brush with the melted butter. Cook for about 40 minutes and dust with icing sugar.

Cheese

WELSH HONEYED CHEESE PÂTÉ WITH WHISKY

Ingredients

150g each of Welsh grated farmhouse cheese and butter
1 tbsp each of local honey and Welsh liqueur whisky or mead
1tsp each of grain mustard and fine fresh chives

Method

Mix all the ingredients together either with a wooden spoon or in a food processor. Remove and place onto some parchment paper or special clingfilm. Roll into a sausage shape and chill or freeze in small 3-inch lengths. Slice and use as required with a good bread or as a starter with a salad garnish.

Welsh hard cheese varieties suitable for this recipe include Nantybwla, Cenarth, Llanboidy, Llangloffan, Celtica and plain Caerphilly.

CHEESEMAKING

Farmers' markets are the places to find wonderful individual artisan dairy products. The markets in France and Brittany are well-known for their cheese. The Bretons have a particular taste for buttermilk. Farmers' cheeses are eaten very fresh, such as *cremet nantais* and *mingaux*, both of which are creamy cheeses with a distinct flavour. *Fromage nantais* is the only aged cheese, sometimes called *fromage du curé*, as it was developed by a priest. Austria and Wales both have a new cheese industry, producing individual farmhouse cheeses.

Wine

THE WINES AND DRINKS OF THE CELTS

There seems to be a unanimous opinion that the Celts loved drinking wine. Plato noted, for example, that 'they craved it and drank it greedily'. Evidence of the trade in wine was extensive along the great wine river valleys – up the Rhone from Marseille, along the Rhine, Danube, Loire, Seine, Meuse, Elbe, even along the Severn. In Champagne the evidence is extensive. The historian John Davies has noted that the Celts moved westwards through acculturation.

Archaeologists working on Celtic Hallstadt discovered evidence of a developed wine-drinking culture. Wine was the mainspring of trade with the Mediterranean, and was transported as a spice concentrate. The wine-drinking culture of Hallstadt was only destroyed after these provinces around the Danube fell to the Romans in 16 BC.

Mead, methaglin and hydromel are the oldest drinks known to have existed and are made from honey and water. Mead is a very old Indo-European word: it is added to wines with pepper and spices.

KELTENWEIN IN AUSTRIA

In Rust on the Neusiedler See, east of Vienna, a winemaker and tireless experimenter called Paul Triebaumer produced Keltenwein ten years ago. This wine was inspired by the discoveries made by local archeologists of grape pips attesting to the use of noble grape varieties in Burgenland long before the arrival of the Romans. A perfectly natural Welschriesling wine was produced. Bottled in corked beer bottles, there is no sulphur in the wine, and it oxidises rapidly on opening.

Appendix

Dumplings

Each Celtic country has its own recipe for dumplings, which are made to accompany soups, main courses or to be served as puddings, dusted with cinnamon and sugar. They can be made very simply from a choice of different flours, potato, semolina, or stale bread cooked plain or with sweet or savoury fillings.

Simple Dumplings – Nockerln (mid-Europe)

Ingredients
    150g flour, 15g melted butter, 1 egg and milk to mix

Method
    Mix all ingredients to a smooth dough and drop dessertspoonfuls into salted boiling water to cook for 15 minutes. Drain and serve in soups or dusted with parsley with a main course.

Clootie Dumplings (Scotland)

Ingredients
    500g each self-raising flour and dried fruit, 125g each of sugar and suet, ½ tsp mixed spice, 1 tbsp treacle and milk to mix

Method
    Mix all the ingredients with the treacle and milk to make a stiff dough. Place in a clean scalded cloth and shape as a sausage. Place in boiling water to cook for 3-4 hours or use a pressure cooker. Serve sliced hot with a sauce or cold as a cake.

Basic Shortcrust Pastry

Ingredients
    225g flour
    75g lard and margarine mixed
    75-100ml cold water

Method
    Rub fat into fine breadcrumbs with
    flour. Mix with water to a soft dough.

Use for pies, pasties pastries, tarts.

Traditional Cornish Pasty

Filling
    225g minced lean beef, 2 sliced
    potatoes, 1 small turnip and 1 onion

Method
    Make shortcrust pastry; divide into two
    and roll into 6-7 inch rounds. Layer the
    vegetables in the centre with the meat
    and onion on top, and season. Brush
    the edges with water and draw togeth-
    er, crimping the edges. Place on baking
    sheet and bake at oven temperature
    230°C for 20 minutes.

Basic White Sauce (sweet or savoury)

Ingredients
    30g each flour and butter, 10 fl oz milk

Method
    Melt the butter and add flour and then
    the milk, gradually stirring over a low
    heat until thickened. Add seasoning
    and herbs such as parsley and other
    ingredients for savoury sauces.
    Sweeten the sauce with sugar or
    honey for desserts.

WEIGHTS AND MEASURES

WEIGHTS		
Metric	UK/US	
15 g		½ oz
30 g		1 oz
45 g		1½ oz
60 g		2 oz
75 g		2½ oz
90 g		3 oz
100 g		3½ oz
125 g	¼ lb	4 oz
150 g	⅓ lb	5 oz
180 g		6 oz
200 g		7 oz
250 g	½ lb	8 oz
300 g		10 oz
350 g	¾ lb	12 oz
500 g	1 lb	16 oz
600 g	1¼ lb	
750 g	1½ lb	
1 kg	2 lb	
1.25 kg	2½ lb	
1.5 kg	3 lb	
2 kg	4½ lb	
2.25 kg	5 lb	

LIQUIDS		
Metric	UK	
60 ml	2 fl oz	
80 ml	3 fl oz	
100 ml	4 fl oz	
125 ml	4½ fl oz	
150 ml	5 fl oz	¼ pt
185 ml	6 fl oz	
200 ml	7 fl oz	⅓ pt
225 ml	8 fl oz	
300 ml	10 fl oz	½ pt
400 ml	15 fl oz	¾ pt
500 ml	18 fl oz	
(568 ml	20 fl oz	1 pt)
700 ml		1¼ pt
750 ml		1⅓ pt
800 ml		1½ pt
1 L		1¾ pt
1.25 L		2 pt
1.3 L		2¼ pt
1.4 L		2½ pt
1.5 L		2⅓ pt
1.8 L		3¼ pt
2 L		3½ pt

LIQUIDS		
Metric	US	
60 ml	¼ cup	
80 ml	⅓ cup	5 tbsp
95 ml		6 tbsp
125 ml	½ cup	
160 ml	⅔ cup	
185 ml	¾ cup	
250 ml	1 cup	
310 ml	1¼ cups	
330 ml	1⅓ cups	
375 ml	1½ cups	
410 ml	1⅔ cups	
435 ml	1¾ cups	
500 ml	2 cups	
560 ml	2¼ cups	
625 ml	2½ cups	
685 ml	2¾ cups	
750 ml	3 cups	
1 L	1 qt	

COMPARATIVE OVEN TEMPERATURES					
°C	°F	gas	°C	°F	gas
140	275	1	200	400	6
150	300	2	220	425	7
160	325	3	230	450	8
175	350	4	240	475	9
190	375	5			